LIFE AT ZERO DISTANCE

The words and concepts expressed here
have been around since the beginning of humankind.
They are not mine, and hence not copyrighted.
This is one of the ways eternal Truth is dancing with us;
therefore the usage or quoting of these texts are entirely
appropriate for any and every purpose whatsoever.

****

Anamika Borst - Auroville 2014

ISBN 9781502732934
IDDN.IN.010.0120029.000.R.P.2014.040.30620

www.anamikaborst.com

LIFE AT ZERO DISTANCE

The freedom of being nothing and none

Anamika Borst

This is not a book on spirituality.

It does not explain how to attain
other levels or higher states.

It has no program to help reach somewhere.

It is merely presenting Life as it is.

Contents

Part 3. Step back

Part 4. Life beyond labels

Part 5. Emptiness

Part 6. Heaven is now

Part 7. When the veils are gone

Part 8. Breathtaking

Part 9. Stripped

Part 10. The ruthless Truth

∞

This is all there is.

What It is we do not know.

We only know that it Is.

All else is story.

Foreword

Here are some pebbles, some pieces of burnt wood from bonfires, some seaweed. For a foreword is a beach shoreline.

A few steps and you are in the ocean of Anamika.

~ ~ ~

Anamika contacted me a few years ago.
We've been corresponding regularly ever since about an unfolding contained in a recognition of what she calls "the staggering immediacy."

The unfolding is unjudged. There is no one to judge it. And, as Anamika says, "No me, no problem."

And at the same time psychological phantoms might appear on the seeker's stage, using judgment and contemplation to try to get a grip on this unfolding.

As all unfolding is contained in the recognition of Immediacy, it is life at zero distance, or what Anamika calls "the natural state" or "life happening."

~ ~ ~

Reading this book, the recognition may crystallize.
It may happen on any page or when you close the book and shut your eyes.

The words or understanding may come forth,
"Oh, I'm not having an experience. I'm not actually
judging, manipulating, or even contemplating
experience. It is all a play. There is only experiencing."

~ ~ ~

The sand gets wet, foam meets your feet, and you see
that if eternity has mass, it is in the form of the ocean.

A few steps and you are the ocean.

Jerry Katz
www.nonduality.org

The first principle

A clear view

This message
can never be understood with the mind.
It is not an intellectual grasping.

It is the end
of all grasping,
of all wanting to get
and to understand.

The end of trying to reach
something,
somewhere,
some state of being.

And it is the end
of the feeling
that something
is wrong or missing
or that something
is out of place.

It is arriving home.
A place we lost sight of,
looking for something else.

The search and the grasping,
the looking for completion and fulfilment
are inherent to being identified
with this contracted energy
we have mistakenly called me.

The place we never left
is the true sense of I
that shines already
through the stories
that thoughts and emotions
are spinning.

This place
is a placeless place,
home.

This is our felt sense
of who we are.

On top of this open Emptiness,
have accumulated over the years
layers and layers of conditioning
that have condensed
into an energetic construct.

A clear view reveals
this erroneous assumption.

We are only Oneness
looking for ourselves.

Lost your glasses?

Stop in your tracks.
Stop for once and notice what is always here.
Notice what is always present in all your experiences.

See that there is a constant stream of things coming
and going.
Thoughts, feelings, sensations, people and happenings.
They all have a beginning and an end, constantly
changing.

Notice that there is something that notices this stream,
something that is always here, unchanging.

This Something is just here.
It is always here.
It is never not here.
Always Present.
The one thing that is constant.
It is so close and natural to us that we fail to notice it.

It is like the fish in the ocean looking for water.

It is like searching for our glasses while all the time we
are looking through them.

We are this timeless always present Awareness.
Already the case.

Vanilla pudding

Throw it all on the garbage heap.
Chuck it out.
All knowledge.
All ideas.
All concepts.
Leave it all behind.

Free from labels.

Can we look upon the world with fresh eyes
as if for the first time?

Not knowing...

Does it have to make sense?

"Here I am."

As Awareness is All,
the ultimate subject,
what All is,
what we all Are,
so everything
we meet is It.

All the contacts with the world
are only ever the Beloved meeting us.
Every face, smell, colour, sound, sensation.
The smiling kid looking up,
the grumpy salesman in the shop,
the embrace of the lover,
the throes of the illness.

No getting away from It.

The Beloved pursues us relentlessly.

Every breath we take
is only ever This
that is touching us
with Itself.

The boredom, the depression,
the delight and the joy.

Through every contact
it is calling out to us:
"Here I am."

Calamity

Opening up to what is,
what we always are
right here,
right now,
the seeking stops.
The search ends.

From a personal point of view, a calamity.
An existence where there are no more goals,
no more ideas or ideals to go after.
The centre of the universe,
the idea of being a person collapses.
And everything that made sense before
is now seen to be empty, meaningless.

But when Existence is pulled free
from this limited point of view,
It reveals itself to itself.

And Life becomes a wondrous happening.
A mysterious unknown
where everything is full of meaning.
Fullness itself without explanations.
The immediacy of perceiving what Is.
The beauty.
The ear-splitting silence.
The peace that passeth all understanding.

The total acceptance of what Is.
Choicelessly aware.

The first principle

The first principle
that on which all else is based
is Consciousness.

Being Conscious,
Conscious Being.

This is before all else appears.
This is what we Are.
The ground of All Being.
And on This and as This
the story of a person unfolds.

To be able to understand This experientially,
we can for instance imagine ourselves
in a room where there is
no light at all,
no sound at all,
no smell at all,
where there are
no sensory stimuli of any kind.

Then when the body is at ease,
and therefore not noticed,
if we push the pause button
on thoughts for a few moments,
what do we notice?

One is.
This is It.

Pristine

Does it matter
to the immaculate unknowable Something
that grogginess and dullness are here?

Does it make a dent
in its unmovable Nature
that there is preoccupation
with family stories?

Does this pristine aware unchanging Space
have an opinion about which movie is being
watched?

It would not be Freedom
if there would be a condition.

It is unconditional Wholeness
and includes all and everything.

All the stories of humanity
are playing out
in This as This.

Stop

When we understand
that the thing or no thing
we are looking for
is already the case
and know intuitively
that seeking is not
bringing us over there,
maybe the time has come
for us to change our strategy.

Stop looking in the mind
for answers.

Stop trying to grasp.

Stop the forward movement
of the me over here
and the something
to get over there.

Stop for a moment
and notice what is present.

Collecting dust

At some point, through insights and or grace,
the impulse might come to stop following,
and to stop believing what other people tell us.

Getting tired with listening to these nondual
guys or girls sitting in front singing their songs?

Not even bothering
to read the latest book
that was ordered out of habit,
and is collecting dust on the table?

Websites and YouTube interviews?
Thousands of hours...
Bored of listening, reading about it?

Who knows?
Some momentum might be gathering
to stop consuming, to stop taking in
more lullabies.
And just look and see.

Where are you reading these words from?
See for yourself
as no one can do this for you.

It is the end of the someone
who is trying to go somewhere.
And only seeing, perceiving is left.

Shape shifter

The fabric of Life

As the play of Life
apparent happenings are going on.
Stories within stories.

All is Consciousness experiencing
itself manifold.

We are taken in by appearances.
It is convincing and enticing.
We love the drama of it.
The wealth of the emotions,
the agonies and the ecstasies.

We have become so hypnotized
by the rich fabric of Life
where every strand is a person with a story
that spins itself into a past and a future,
that we have lost sight of That in which
all is unfolding.

That Is has no name,
is timeless,
sees all the stories,
their beginnings
and their endings,
and remains.
That is what we are
beyond all the labels
and the stories.

Be still and Know the I Am.

A case of mistaken identity

Doubtlessly knowing who we are,
innately, without form or object.

Feeling whole and complete.

An openness that
is unmoving
is not rejecting,
is not reaching out.

This is our natural state
that becomes apparent
once the belief in the person subsides.

Once the true identity
has been seen and taken on,
erroneous beliefs fall away.

Like a house of cards.

All problems of existence are there
because of a case of mistaken identity.

When there is no person as a reference,
it is just Life happening.

The lynchpin

The lynchpin
on which all of our misconceptions hang
is the construct of
and belief in being a someone.

All felt sense of separation,
of not being there yet,
of levels and goals to reach
are hinged on this one core notion.

If it falls away,
through investigation,
it is seen that it was never real.

It is like a castle in the air
apparent for some time
and interesting to watch
but when blown away,
only empty sky is left.

Just a game

Naming, labelling comes after the fact.
Comes after perceiving.
It happens so fast that it mostly goes unnoticed.

Before we comprehend the babbling noises
adults direct at us, tiny tots still, everything is
perceived without filters.
We are aware of all the sensory perceptions
directly.

Then language comes into being.
Everything that is perceived immediate
and as non-separative from the perceiving
becomes a something with a name.

We end up living in the illusion
of being a someone perceiving the world through
naming and labelling, while it is just a game.
Awareness is there before the game starts.

Find out your natural state, your original face.

What is before any object makes an appearance?
What is before a supposed someone divides it up
into this and that?

There is only One.
The perceiving.
The person we think ourselves to be
is an illusion.

Fields with crops

Early morning.

The sun appearing over grey heavy clouds.
A vast landscape with the tops of trees
and a solitary church steeple
sticking out of the fog that hugs the ground.
The road winds its way on top of the dike.
The fragrance of freshly cut grass.
Birds, sheep, fields with crops,
green everywhere, and water.

An endless vastness.
A gentle peace pervading all.

In nature it is easy to feel
that Existence has no boundaries.
No separateness.
It is one movement.

All happening in what we are.
As it is.

It is when we bump into human life
that we are seemingly confronted with others.
With what appears to us as limitations and boundaries.
Strong personalities evoking reactions.
Demands and expectations of our surroundings.

It is our own belief in being a person
that makes it appear so.

These demands and reactions
rub against what we believe to be a me.

When the belief drops away,
we see that these apparent limitations
have no reality.

It is not that reactions or demands
are not felt and noticed.
They are seen in clarity
but as they have nothing to hold on to,
they are gone in no time,
just passing by.

Everything
appears in this vast space
and disappears without a trace.

Investigating this apparent me is the key.
The key to the gateless gate.

New

The unimaginable newness of each moment.

The unborn, the unmanifest perceives Itself
through all our senses at each moment.
At each moment It tastes, sees, hears, senses
through what we think of
as our eyes, our ears, our taste buds, our skin.

Just for a moment, imagine...

There is only the Divine
as there is nothing else but That.
So where does this leave us?

The hypnosis of being a person is in reality
That living and perceiving through us, as us.
Whether we are aware of this or not
does not make any difference.
It is happening anyway.

When the illusion of being a limited person
is seen through,
we know that there is only This
expressing and experiencing Itself
through and as all appearances and stories.

Opening up to This as This
we are touched by beauty, joy and gratitude.

The wonder and aliveness of each moment.

Shape shifter

When we say we are a person,
what we actually speak of
is a combination
of an energetic contraction
and unexamined ideas.

A person makes it sound
like something
solid,
independent,
separate.

While if we look closely
it is an ever shifting blend of
memories,
habits,
reactions,
convictions,
wishes,
aversions,
opinions
that are mostly not questioned
but that change whenever we do.

And this is connected to a body
that has been changing shape
ever since it made its appearance.

It is all those believed ideas
that keep the energetic contraction in place.

Home base

Whatever happened to our natural curiosity,
our childlike wondering?

Not yet fallen out of paradise.
Still one with all that is perceived.

All the questions naturally coming up
when entering this wondrous world.

What is This?
What is a colour, a shape
so marvelous to behold?
Too beautiful to put away with a label.

Where has it gone?
And when did it make place
for the limitations and fixed ideas
that made of Life
a cardboard box of reality?

Hard, thin and superficial.
Making us feel separate and alienated.
Trying so hard to fit into society.

Adjust, obey, be a good girl or boy.
Don't upset the structures in place.

No wonder there are so many walking around
feeling lost, feeling like misfits, depressed.

Because it is just not possible to find
true and lasting happiness
in pursuit of all that has been dangled
in front of our nose.

Paradise is always present.

Before we started to believe the stories
of everyone around us.

Through a cacophony
of conditioning, ideas and assumptions,
shines the beauty of that home base.

Never lost and never found
as it could go nowhere.

What if...

What if we always were
the wholeness,
the fullness,
the aliveness...

What if, even if we do not feel it,
we were already whole and complete...

What if we could trust this message
because it resonates
with something inside us already...

And because the one saying these words
inspires confidence.

And an unshakeable permanence
unheard of in this world of shifting shapes
filters down through the words.

What if because of this trust in the message
a bridge were built between what is
and what appears to be...

And we followed naturally the way back home.

What if...

Life without stories

So interesting to see that the person we think
we are is only held up by all the stories we keep
telling ourselves.

I am so and so, have such a character, these
habits.
My likes and dislikes, my inclinations, my
history, my past, my traumas, my goals and my
dreams about the future.

And we keep the stories alive by believing in
them, telling them to others, dwelling on them,
over and over again.

Basically what we do by believing in these
stories is construct the little robot, the person,
the me.

See the amazing creative power
of Consciousness at work.

So what happens when we stop believing in the
stories and stop telling them to others?
And when we see that the repetitive thoughts
are just streams of thoughts that do not have any
reality beyond the value we give them?

What remains without stories?
Aren't you curious?

And who wants to know?

Outside the box

Why not question one's own assumptions?
Why not think outside the box?
Why aim for certainty
when constant change is all we have?

Nothing in the universe,
nothing in one's own experience and perception
ever stays the same.

Watch how the mind tries in vain
to work towards lasting aims.
How it tries again and again
to come up with schemes and charts
to outline and predict
what is unpredictable,
fresh and new
each
time.

And as the mind is doing its thing,
sensations, emotions, moods, thoughts,
perceptions, sounds, colours, shapes and forms
are passing by
in an unending stream.

Endless stories

Going through the day,
just notice that each and every conversation
is a story about something.

Something that happened in the past
or that will happen in the future.
What happened to others, to family or friends.

It is about aches and pains,
with all the details, intricacies
where we dig out and emphasize
how someone was wrong
or something went wrong.

Or about the solutions
through which all the problems of the world,
or our lives, or of society would be solved,
if only they would listen,
if only they knew.

And while all the focus is on the stories
and our reactions to the stories told,
notice that it all relates to something
that is not happening now, in this moment.

Living in our stories,
we miss the immediacy
and the endless wonder of things.

Step back

Aum

The believed-in person has no independent existence.
And can therefore be said to be unreal.

'Reality is that which stands on its own'.

Then we can conclude that there is no need,
or even no possibility to get rid of the person.
As how can we get rid of something
that does not exist in the first place?

A certain amount of energy in the shape of beliefs,
thoughts and convictions have gone into the forming
of this pseudo-identity.

These thoughts and beliefs have contracted and
crystallised into what we believe ourselves to be.
Existing on our own, full of limitations and somewhere
located.

The thing needed to untie the knots of identification
is to see for ourselves the unreality of the person.

That All one ever Is,
is boundless,
ever present
and connected to All and everything.

Omniscient, omnipotent and omnipresent.
Aumniscient, aumnipotent and aumnipresent.

Aum

Nomenomynomine

The one thing blocking clear Seeing
is the belief in the thought
that there is a person.

This spins out as a continuous
self referencing.
Everything is related
to this fictitious entity.

Me, my, mine.
My thoughts, my opinions.

Instead of passing thoughts
appearing and disappearing.

My feelings.
What I feel.
Oh my my...

Instead of emotions
coming and going.

Everything comes and goes
in the same way as the landscape passes by
when we sit in a car.
Trees, people, perceptions, thoughts.
Seen coming and seen going.
No difference.

Centre stage

Information comes in each moment.

Through all the senses,
hearing,
seeing,
tasting,
smelling,
touching
perceiving is ongoing.
It is direct and immediate.
It is happening now.

It is on automatic and in the background.
We pay little attention to it because
we have given thoughts centre stage.

Absorbed by its own stories,
mind endlessly comments
about things already past
or things that have not yet happened.
Always out of tune with now.
Around this we have built an identity.
This is 'me'.

Lopsided we go through Life
sensing something not quite right.

And as the mind and thoughts are accustomed
to go out and look for answers,
that is where the solution is thought to be found.

The mind trying to figure out its own demise,
while all the while the solution is where we are.

Seeing, perceiving always ongoing
in the immediacy of Presence.

There never was a blockage.
There never was a closed door.
Only a thinking identity
mistaking itself as separate.

It is a matter of noticing the fallacy of thoughts
and all the stories they tell.

They bear no more weight
than clouds moving in front of the sun.

When they vanish into thin air,
the Vastness is revealed.

Who I am?

I know who I am.
It is not this person.

I know who I am.
And it is not visible.

I know what I am.
Still it is not anything anyone ever called me.

I know what I am.
Though it is impossible to put it into words.

I know who I am.
But It is nothing tangible.

I know who I am.
It is not here or there,
yet closer than my own breath.

Preferences

Given a choice,
most would prefer
to be comfortable
than to be free.

But as there is no one
to have a choice,
the preference
for not upsetting the status quo,
for not investigating the belief
of being a separate limited individual,
is also just happening.

Oneness playing the game
of not wanting to recognize itself.

Yet?

C'est la Vie!

One common misunderstanding is that once we have
reached, Life looks different, more beautiful.
There is an intensity, a strong sense of presence.

It is true there are such moments and days that this is
presenting itself.
And then a few days, a few hours later, the following
morning, the intensity is gone.
Everything looks same old, same old...
And the person is under the illusion that it has been
lost while there has never been a person to reach
anything in the first place.

This is where the confusion is.
A confusion of identity.

If we know ourselves to be the open aware presence,
all unfolds in what we are.
How can something be lost if we are It?

Everything appears in what we are.
Also the headache and irritation on waking up,
also the weariness and tiredness in the body.

Nothing is ever not seen by what we are.
Nothing is ever excluded by what we are.

We are the open aware space
in which Everything comes and goes.
C'est la vie!

Bicycle

All good pointers bring the seeker after the pot
of gold, the voracious reader to the one place
overlooked.

The very place where the reader and seeker
is seeing from.
The placeless place where you are right now
reading these words from.

Anything else is taking you for a ride.
Just investigate.

Where are you right now?
Where do the questions pop up in?
Who is looking?

Do not believe or follow anyone.
Dismiss all concepts.
Follow your intuition, investigate, find out.

You are the answer to your seeking.

And of course a bicycle has nothing to do
with anything.
Just as pointers and teachers are equally
redundant after reaching the destination.

Thanks for the ride...

I am the place I never left.

Prison

How come
when we question and lament our prison,
we never consider questioning the prisoner?

It is our mistaken identification
with the person, the prisoner,
that is the cause of all felt limitations.

Limitations are inherent to being a person.

But we are,
all of us,
God having a human experience.

Know who and what we are
and what we are not.
Then all perceived limitations are noticed
as part of the play of Life,
to add colour and spice to Existence.

When identification drops away,
our natural state becomes apparent.

What we are is
inherently limitless.

What a relief...

One huge benefit, after recognizing
that this perspective is who we are,
is the dropping away of the sense of lack.

We are home.

The feeling that something is wrong is gone.

The drive to improve this imperfect person
chasing after a perfection always out of reach
falls away.

What a relief...

Immutably so

The one stable factor in your life,
in anyone's life, is the you
who is watching, seeing, experiencing this life.

In other words,
you see life happening.

It appears as shapes and forms,
colours and sounds,
smells and tastes,
thoughts and sensations.

This life is in constant flux,
always changing.

The one who is noticing however
is always the same.
It is always you.

Immutably so.
Not going anywhere.
Always right here, right now.

Life appears in what you are,
this open spacious Awareness.

And you are the Life
that is appearing in you as you
for no separation is to be found.

Allowing

What if we are never separate in the first place?

What if the energetic contraction felt at this
moment is just a temporary suit and masks what
we agree to wear at a masked ball?

And then we forget that it is just a party
and keep on wearing this persona.
Pretending to be so and so.
Everyone playing a game.
Cases of mistaken identity.

What if we allow the possibility to be felt,
the perfume to enter
that we are just actors in our own movie?

The realization might dawn
that we are not this person with this story?

What if we can perceive of the possibility that
we are the screen, the props and the characters
appearing?
The walls, the smells, the sights and the sounds?
And we are also the One watching the movie?

In fact there is nothing outside of what I am.

What if this is already how it is?

What if?

Step back

Consent to be nothing and none, dissolve Time's work,
Cast off thy mind, step back from form and name.
Annul thyself that only God may be.

— SRI AUROBINDO

Step back.
Step back.

Back from the motivation to act.

From the identification
with the swirling thoughts
and lingering feelings
passing by like buses and cars
in front of our window.

Back from everything
that defines us as a person.

Step back from everything
that tells us that we are limited and separate.

Step back just a little while
as if it were a game we play.

When we came into the world, we played the game of
being the little child because we so much needed to
please. Our survival depended on it.

After playing the game of being this little girl
or boy for some time, we forgot that it was just
a game because no one told us otherwise.

And with this forgetting we lost home,
not knowing any more who we truly are.

Instead, we identified with this pseudo-identity
always sensing something is not quite right,
something is missing, something is wrong.

And like everyone else, we started to look
outward, somewhere else for completion.
Relationships, work, money, enlightenment,
cats and dogs, children, cigarettes, sex, drugs,
and rock 'n' roll.

Anything at all to fill up the hole created by this
misidentification.

We lost sight of the simple fact of Being.
Unconditionally present.
Always here and now.
And more intimate than our own breath.

Step back.
And see what is present already...

Life beyond labels

Freedom

Blessed freedom
from all conventions, morals and expectations.

The freedom from the notion
that we should conform and fit in.

The freedom to be
whatever is expressing itself at this moment.

That can be anything.
From sweet and compassionate
to upset and even slightly mad.
As there is no one to check or even to know
what the next action or thought is going to be.

The freedom also from the idea
that what is written here
should be coherent or intelligent.
As there is never an idea
of what is going to come.

It is liberation from the person
that is freedom from limitations.

Basically

Knowing
who and what one is
means basically
that one lives in unknowing.

No clue really
as it cannot be grasped.

But one knows that one is.
One is aware
and knows when one is aware.

This is freedom.
Freedom from beliefs and illusions.
Freedom from the weight of the past.
From so and so said so,
and from stale reverence.
From habits and empty rituals
that have replaced
the living questions that brought us here.

Life is living and moving,
always fresh and new.

As soon as we label it, bottle it,
put a lid on it and shelve it to be adored,
Life has passed us by already.

What do we know?

What do we know?
What is knowledge?

Is it all that is gathered and has accumulated during
our lifetime, imparted to us by parents and society?

How to behave and to speak,
education,
the facts of Life
and which ideals to follow.

We repeat what they told us like trained monkeys.

As children fallen out of paradise,
believing the falsehood of separation
because no one told us otherwise.
What choice did we have?
Trained monkeys we are, all of us.

Shining through this veneer of 'civilisation' is
a raw vitality.
Life itself.
What we are, as there is no separation.

Who and what were we before our training began?
Before conditioning started?
What is our original face?

No clue

The person I believed myself to be
had always been good at hiding.

Disappearing into the woodwork
had been her life motto:
"They might discover I am a fake,
that I have no clue what is going on."

Now Awareness has taken over
and those tendencies get overruled.

As Awareness loves to play.
Sees itself in all the contacts of the world.
Loves to break limitations.
Tumbles over borders.
Nudges at firmly held beliefs.
Bursts out laughing at so called problems
and delights in recognizing Itself.

Calling out to all and everyone:
"Look, I am you,
you are me,
there is only One."

Crickets chirp.
A ticking clock.
In the distance some thunder.
The humid atmosphere of a tropical evening.

 And still no clue what is going on.

The great Unknown

Nothing is certain in this relative world.
Except the fact that everything comes and goes.

All we are holding on to as mine includes: my family,
my friendships, my home, my possessions, my work,
my character, my body, my abilities, my progress, my
ego, my spiritual path, my surrender...

The certainties that give stability to our lives
are always subject to change and can be taken away
at any time at a moment's notice.

One tsunami and all is swept away.
One accident and our lives are in turmoil.
One brain tumour and the person we thought
ourselves to be has changed beyond recognition.

Nothing will change this fact.
The great Unknown is the base of our existence.
Is what we are.

When it dawns on us that in the relative world,
we will never find the permanency we are searching
for, we might be ready for a new adventure.
Our next quest...
The certainty of the Absolute in which all takes place.

Is there any way to get to This?
And who is asking?

54

Dancing Mountain

Is there any certainty?

Is there anything in our lives
stable or constant?

Apparently everything is in motion.
Cells in our bodies are formed
and die in their millions every second.

Whatever we perceive
is in a process of change.

Even a mountain
so solid and unmovable is dancing.

Pushed up by eruptions and continental plates,
it is expanding.
Or through erosion,
it is shrinking before our undiscerning eyes.

To find security in the world is a delusion.

The only constant is change.

And what about That
that notices these changes?

What is looking, noticing?

Life beyond labels

An invitation to step out of the known,
of everything that is safe and comfortable.

Are you tired of the felt limitations?
Always the same habitual responses coming up?
Does Life seem too predictable?
Is Life always same old, same old?

The known projects itself forward into sizable chunks.
Labels everything that comes in.
Has opinions and judgments about all information.
And rarely questions these assumptions.

Is there not secretly somewhere a longing to step out
of this mold?

Where is the miraculous, the open space, the freedom?

How strange that we are never taught to turn our
attention to the direct contact where our attention
meets sights, smells, tastes, touches and sounds.

We are only ever taught to notice the labels.
It is green, it is grass, it is food for the cows.
It is white, it is cold, it is snow.
It is red, it has thorns, it is a rose.

Soon we live in a world of ideas, a paper thin
construction.

Only touching this artificial structure where all is
known, rarely perceiving without it, we bypass
the bare Aliveness.
Life without ideas.
The Unknown.

Life beyond labels is a life without this identity.
It is the direct cognition with what is appearing
at exactly this moment.

Without ideas, with direct perception,
there is no person operating.

It is Life experiencing Itself.

Flapping in the wind

Quiet Sunday morning.
The washing hanging on the terrace.
T-shirts flapping in the wind.
The clanging sound of the windmill.
Sunlight shining impartially on all.

Where is the need to define?
To analyse and extract?
Do we need to use the mind to go to a no-mind place?

"Thought cannot transcend thought," says Francis
Lucille.

Then how does recognition take place?

Can we see now without using mind or thought
that there is in our experience already a functioning,
an ability to see clearly, to know without thoughts?

A knowledge through identity?

Attention makes contact with something and knows
it by sensing it, being it because there is already no
distance.

It is not something to achieve.

It is not somewhere to go.

It is not an understanding that is lacking.

It is plain seeing
without the use of thought.

To realize that the place of not knowing
is already where we are.

Everything appears miraculously
and is known.

Presence beyond belief

What is the truth
of Existence,
of Life,
of Ourselves?

Can we capture it in words and concepts?

Measuring the Infinite with yardsticks?
Taking a bucket of water to describe the ocean?

What if...

What if right here and right now,
there is no need for words and concepts
to perceive what is already present?

Unclutch the mind
with its persistent habit to grasp.
Just take a look and see.

Presence beyond belief.

Simply here already.

Words can point towards
but never capture the Infinite.
And there is no need
for words to know what we are.

Just this...

Not knowing

Not knowing.
Not sure of anything.
The world of things
of mine and thine is a mystery.

A web of interpretations
has covered the unfathomable.

Cut into little pieces
that imagine
that each lives as if it has a life of its own.

Split from the origin,
pretending that the world is known
by its labels.

Dried up, stick like,
living lives of quiet desperation.

Step beyond the labels
and fall into the bottomless
ocean of Being.

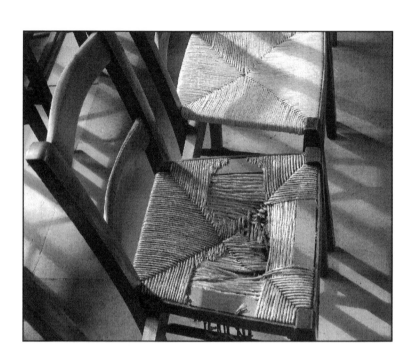

Emptiness

How on earth?

How on earth do we figure out our existence?
What is Life?

If we are lucky enough,
this question will take hold of us.
And break through the comfort zone
of an ordered and predictable existence.

Dismantle the imaginary boundaries
that have hypnotized us and lead us to believe
there is a separation
between the perceiver and the perceived.

If we are lucky enough,
this question will break us open.
Leave us bare, empty.
And remove identifications
until Reality is seen
and all questions leave us.

There are no answers.

We are,
Life is the answer.

Form is Emptiness.
Emptiness is Form.

No one at home

One big blank.
An empty screen.
Letters are appearing.
Fingers are tapping.
A lizard's call is heard.

By Whom?

Is there any One?

Is this not just all appearing
in the Oneness,
in the One space?

No division between
sound and listening,
sight and seeing.

No one at home.

All there is
is knowing Emptiness.

Benevolence

The benevolence
of this Perspective
of what is.

The touching,
seeing,
knowing
of All that is.

A colour green, blue, red overwhelms.
The heart wrenching story of a friend.
The touch of a crayon on paper.
The movement of a hand.
A ray of sunlight dancing on a knee.

Tears in one's eyes
for everything
for nothing.

The unbearable openness of Being.
And knowing no other way to be.

Total vulnerability.
Availability.

Emptiness.

It scares the hell...

What are we without our story?
What becomes most obvious?

Life is empty, plain and boring.
Just perceiving without a me.

And it scares the hell out of us.
Emptiness swallowing up the story of a me.

What is left of this person?
This person with a history, a future,
a personality?

Nothing at all is left.

It is like a tight fist opening up.
Allowing.
Not grasping.
Not wanting things to be different.
And noticing that without a story,
Life just is...

In this Isness of Life,
without the story,
meaning without the person,
there is no separation
between perceptions and the perceiver.

It is Emptiness perceiving.

Moaning about shackles

When Oneness
is making itself felt within a human story,
it is often in the guise of a calamity:
an accident,
a severe disease,
the loss of a dear one,
being laid off work,
depression,
anything that may send us into the pit.

And all this coming out of nowhere.
Ripping apart
the well manicured borders of our existence.

Suddenly confronted with the Unknown,
the Emptiness,
the depth of the abyss.
And the agonizing knowledge
that nothing in our education
and our upbringing,
in fact nothing in our lives,
has prepared us for this.

Where to turn?

How to manage this onslaught of debilitating
and terrifying energies and emotions?

Emptiness,
this aware and intelligent presence shakes itself
just a bit to free itself of some of the shackles
that have covered up its existence.

As on a chess board,
eliminate a few of the personas
we have identified with over the years:
the savvy intellectual,
the miserable seeker,
the eminent scholar,
the poor me...
the great me...
to make room for recognition to take place.

And yes, this might feel painful and hurt in the
beginning, like shedding a skin and having to
confront life in a vulnerable and raw manner.

But why not look around in this unfamiliar
space?
And look Emptiness right in the face?

We might find that suddenly we are at home
just then and there.

Who moans about the shackles left behind when
stepping through the prison door to freedom?

Emptiness

We are all empty.
Open to receive whatever happens to be
in our field of perception.
At each moment, this is already happening
and for every one.

Now the aspect of Emptiness
might not be obvious for most
as we are so absorbed by the identification with one
fragment of all appearances.
And that is the person we think we are.

Without questioning this reference point built up over
decades, reinforced and confirmed by society, friends,
family, the whole freaking world, we do not notice this
open empty aware Something.
Already there seeing, perceiving.
Every little and amazing thing happening.

Rattle the cage.
Dare to question everything that tells you
that you are limited and separate.

What we are is no thing.
Unidentifiable.

An open perceiving capacity
and at the same time
All that appears.

Sinking slowly

Late afternoon a magpie robin sings while the
sun is sinking slowly behind the trees.

Rays of sunlight colouring the living room
in deep yellow-orange.

Two young mongooses running over the terrace
looking up when they hear the tapping from the
laptop.

The wind coming in through the windows
caresses the skin.

Perceiving is ongoing at all times.
One knows a thought.
One knows a sensation, a feeling.
One knows a sound, a form, a shape.

Cognizing what is.
Without words.
Always happening.

One describes and labels to communicate.
But always with the understanding
that there is no separate person doing it.

The perceiving is never apart
from what is perceived.

It is Emptiness cognizing.

Heaven is now

Only This

This pulsating Aliveness.
Ever present.
No limits.
No borders.
Natural.
Simple.

No big deal.

You in the most You sense possible.
So intimately known.
The only Thing known.

You will always meet only This.
As This is all there is.
And This is You.
Whatever arises.
Whatever appears.

It is only Yourself you meet.
No strangers in YouLand.
Cannot get out of It.
Nowhere to run.
Nothing to get.
You are Here already.
Always.
All.
No you no me.

Only This.

Hopeless

This is hopeless.

For the person to make it into a strategy
and try to grasp or get hold of.

For the mind to understand,
figure out or make it into a system.

The person will never be able to do anything
to come closer.

Really really hopeless...

Nothing you can do.

And then maybe it dawns
that it is a relaxing into That,
what you already are.

A giving up,
a surrender of all grasping and seeking.

Perhaps turn around.
And simply notice
what is here.

Already.
Present.
Always.

Now

Aware Presence.

What we are
is always
alive,
immediate,
fresh.

It is not then and there
but now and here
totally available and open.

And only so
because it is recognized
now and now and now.

Again and again.

That is the Aliveness,
the recognition of the moment.

At each moment,
as there is only ever now.
With all the senses wide open.

Dynamite

Dark quiet night.
Hooting scops owl.
Toothpick between teeth.
Uncomfortable sensations.
Barking dogs in the distance.
Fragrance of incense.

Not feeling the need to spread the word.

And in the world of separation
where the idea of being a person is believed,
no one wants to hear this.
No one wants to dynamite one's own house.

No one will get this anyway.

It is just noticing all the sense perceptions
taking place automatically,
without a someone doing it.
Already ongoing.
Every moment.
Effortlessly.

Just singing my song...

Knowing

It is the quiet noticing of everything.

Not only a noticing,
it is also a knowing.

A knowing of everything that appears.

A wordless recognition
whereby a dog is known as a dog
and not as an apple pie.

This knowing is instant and immediate.
Knowledge through identity.

It is prior to labelling and judging.
Prior to our hopes and fears.

That dog is big.
It is probably an angry dog.
I hope it will not bark.

It is before the mind kicks in
and spins its stories.

It is the noticing
of whatever presents itself.

The puppet

Awareness shines its light
on everything that appears.

Thoughts and feelings.
Imagination and dreams.
The sublime and the mundane.
The beautiful and the hideous.
The exciting and the boring.

All qualities and expressions possible.

The beggar in the street.
The newlyweds.
The sinner and the saint.

Nothing is excluded.

This amazing dance of possibilities,
movements, creative outpourings.

Awareness knows it all
and sees it all coming into
and going out of Existence.

When Awareness comes to know Itself,
not as the puppet at the mercy
of the ups and downs of Life,
but as That in which all is happening,
there is the joy of union,
the intimacy of a lover's embrace with Existence.

Awaring

Once this is seen,
the looking out of our eyes,
which is no big deal
as it is our experience always
and so for everyone,
we might wonder, a bit bewildered:
"Now what? Is this all there is to it?"

And yes it is.
But the catch is that it is not a state.
It can be confusing
as the word Awareness is a noun.
So in language, it becomes an object,
something the person reaches out to
and wants to achieve or understand.
While actually This is not a thing.
It is more an activity,
an ongoing noticing.

So a verb is more accurate.
Awaring.

Once this is seen,
keep seeing,
keep awaring,
keep noticing that.

This is always happening.
It is the only happening.

Seeing, awaring always ongoing.
Always the only thing going on.

Thoughts, feelings and sensations
are appearing and disappearing
in the immediacy of seeing and noticing.

This is the only thing
that is real and constant.

And in this immediate seeing,
there is no person.

Thoughts about the person
come and go in this.

We need to keep seeing this
again and again,
awaring of this until it sinks in
that this is all there ever is.
Everything else comes and goes.

Then it dawns
that actually this is
what we are,
the Awaring,
the Seeing,
the Knowing.

Footsteps on cobbled streets

Sitting in an apartment
in the heart of Amsterdam.
Overlooking a canal lined with boats and trees.
A canal cruise full of tourists is passing by
leaving a wake in the water.
Tiny eddies catching the sun
in a flickering play of light and shadow.

A door slams and workmen's voices are heard.
Footsteps on cobbled streets.

A man in front of the house
tries to figure out the parking ticket machine.
Cycles with big chains and locks
clustered here and there.

A tap drips and an airplane flies over.
The taste of coffee in the mouth
and a sensation of warmth.

Colours and shapes.
Noises and sounds.
Tastes and smells.

The body moves as one leg starts to feel numb.
Fingers on the keyboard tapping.

There is no intention.
Merely an observing.

A thought about lunch appears
and disappears again.
No action results as there is no appetite.
A feeling of peace and quietness is present.

Thoughts and feelings.
Sensations and perceptions.

Wherever you are,
there you are.

One seamless totality
in which all takes place.

All happening spontaneously.
No one doing anything.
Life happening.

Where on earth?

Where on earth are we at home?

Is it in a location with favourable circumstances?

Do we need
to strive for these ever changing variables?

The right place,
the right climate,
the right working place,
the right spiritual atmosphere,
the right friends,
the right relationship,
the right social contacts,
the right...

This sounds like a full time job
with the prospect
that the place called Home
escapes us again and again.

Endlessly we try
to put the right pieces together.
And they fall
in and out of harmony
continuously.

There is always something to improve.
Never quite right.

When as a child
our identity shrank
from no separation to the body-mind,
we fell out of paradise.

Lost the one place
that was ours
and settled for a make-believe story.

The story of a person
who lives in
a world full of separate objects.

It is the identification
with being a person
that locks us out of paradise.

Home is the natural state
and already what we are.

Coppersmith

Good morning.
Good morning.
Isn't it a good morning?
Just good to be here?

A walk in the forest.
The rhythm of footsteps
in and out of sync
with a pair of coppersmiths
calling out to each other.

With each branch and twig,
a tiny stone lodged in the shoe,
each intake of breath,
jasmine flowers growing wild
are calling out.

Inviting.

For the joy of It.

With all the senses wide open,
perceiving,
celebrating,
always
happening.

Obviousness

The obviousness
of this perspective is amazing.

It screams at us
as every sound and taste,
every thought and feeling
and every sight and touch.

Happening
through all the senses already.

The preoccupation with the story,
with keeping up the self-image is so absorbing
and so much work
that we lose sight
of this plain and very simple fact.

Nothing we need to do for this.
Nothing we need to achieve.

This is all there is.

It is discovering and recognizing
that it is never not here.
And is happening as all there is.

A bug in the system

Our views and perceptions, thoughts and feelings
are already nondual, direct and immediate.

Already just happening, appearing and noticed.

They are already known for what they are.
Are already totally welcomed and accepted.
As this is what is happening.

Our views and perceptions, thoughts and feelings
do not need permission or acknowledgment to do
what they do.
Which is just appearing the way they do.

It is what is happening.

The apparent person is in no way needed or necessary
for any functioning to take place the way it does.

As with babies, young children and animals.
Life is happening just fine.

The person is an afterthought.
A bug in the system.

A virus that has put an apparent screen
between the perceptions and the cognizing function.

And calls this me.

Happening after the fact.
Out of sync.

And this is also noticed.

There is only nondual perception.
Or if you will, this mysterious happening.
As This is all there is.

This includes always All.
It is the totality.

And in This and as This,
the dance of Life plays out.

A person-centered existence
is simply an aberration of perception
as in reality nothing is ever separate.

Heaven and Hell

Soft silver dew on grass.
An animal snatched
one of my shoes
from the terrace last night.

Amidst a chorus of tweeting birds,
the cawing of crows.

Cool air comes in through the open windows.
And the infection on my heel throbs and oozes.

The gentle morning sun
becomes the murderous fiend at noon.

Whichever way we turn,
there is no up without down.

No good without bad.

Heaven and Hell
sleeping sweetly
on the same pillow.

Heaven is Now.

There is only this moment.

We are under the impression
that this moment is not good enough.

The world is going down
and we need to work hard
to make it a better place.

"I still notice egoistic tendencies in me.
They should not be there.
It should be all already surrendered to the
Divine.
There is still something wrong with me."

We come up with all kinds of arguments
to support our belief that this moment is lacking.

It is an innate sense of unease,
something so close and stuck to us
that we do not even notice it.
Except that it tells us
that this moment is not enough.

It sets us off on all kinds of projects to improve,
to seek solutions,
to labour and sweat
because in the future it will be better.

But this future never arrives.

It is in moments of happiness
of being stunned into Oneness
through falling in love or through Grace,
that we notice that this sense of unease has left us.

We are fully in the present moment.
And we want more of it
because it feels so good.

But once we fall again
down from the heights of happiness,
we even have more arguments
to support our idea that there is something
out there for us to reach.

The golden pot at the end of the rainbow.
Some kind of Heaven.

But, if we pause to consider...

Now is all we have.
There is nothing else.

All ideas about a someone
who has to improve,
about a world
that has to improve,
only happen as ideas in this moment.

Without ideas of something wrong,
there is the immediate sensing
going on effortlessly.

And in this noticing,
unease might be there
or a slight irritation.

All of Life shows its many moods
and everything is noticed and passes.

It passes as there is not a someone
who hooks onto the idea that it should be
different, who keeps perpetuating the story
and the sense of unease.

The simplicity and immediacy are staggering.
The result is an effortless noticing
of everything that occurs.

Welcome to Heaven!

When the veils are gone

No problem

Being aware of being aware,
complications cease.
Problems disappear.

How come?

A problem only exists for a person.

Thoughts spin a story
as they connect an issue
to an imaginary me.

No me.
No problem.

Reality

Spirituality, like all words, is a concept.
We do not know exactly what it is
but we have endowed it
with all kinds of meanings.
And for every person
it represents something different.

Higher states of consciousness.
Hours of meditation to reach enlightenment.
The assuming of an attitude
of aloofness and holiness.
The belief in a deeper and higher reality.
Devotion for deities, gods and gurus.

The list is long.

And yes, it is all in the realm of possibilities
in the story of humanity.

What is talked about here is something different.
It is looking at what is real.
Without concepts and beliefs.

Reality as defined in a dictionary:
'Something that exists
independently of all other things
and from what all other things derive'.

Simply looking what is.

Life perceiving Itself.

No inside, no outside

Ticking of the clock.
A croaking frog.

Sounds appearing and disappearing.

Blinking of the cursor on the screen.
Toes of the right foot on the floor.

Sights and sounds, and sense perceptions.

Itching of the lower lip.
A coconut falling.

Nothing special going on.

Firecrackers in a distant village.
Sounds from the neighbour's house.

Always the same space where it all happens.

Humming of the laptop.
Water drops dripping on the leaves.

It is always here and now.

A thought about work passes by.
The neighbour whistles a little.

Everyone's every moment's perceptions.
And there is no one doing it.

Sensation of heaviness in the shoulders.
Flying foxes flapping their wings in the trees.

No inside, no outside.

A deep sigh...
Tapping of the keys on the keyboard.

No one thing is more mine than the other.
All is of equal importance.

The fridge starts humming.

All sounds equally impassively registered.

A brainfever bird calls.
The stomach rumbles.

Things happening effortlessly.

Firecrackers in crescendo.
Wind rustling the palm leaves.

No doer in sight.

Itching on the left index finger.
A scops owl hooting.

As it is.

Seeing, Knowing

The knowing referred to here
is already operating in every one.

This knowing is immediate and effortless.

It is the direct perceptions through the senses.

Without it, no body-mind could function in this world.

This knowing is not an intellectual knowledge,
thinking things over, forming an opinion.

It is not an encyclopedia of facts that we can bring
forth at timely moments.

It is not the Akashic records that mysteriously
drop down and make us spout utterances
of past lives and future events.

This knowing is the immediate noticing of all
that is present.

That is always operating whether we notice this
consciously or not.

It is knowing without a doubt at every moment
the perceptions of hearing, tasting, seeing, smelling
and touching.

The moment food comes into the mouth,
immediately we know,
without labelling it as such,
whether the food is
hot or cold, salty or sweet,
smooth and soft or crisp and chunky.

No one needs to tell us that.

It is the immediate knowing,
without labelling it as such,
of a splitting headache
or tickling sensations on the foot.
Whether there is a sense of wellbeing,
a bout of depression
or some irritations.

No one needs to tell us that.

It is the immediate effortless knowing
of all that comes in through the senses.

It is as simple as that.

Appearing in the immediacy of Presence
of what we are.

Just this.

Understanding is all.

Understanding is all.
                    - NISARGADATTA MAHARAJ

Can we conceive of the possibility
that what is happening right now
is already the Fullness, the Aliveness?

If we hear that we are That already,
that It is already the case,
that we are never separate from It
because we are It,
then what more needs to happen
to experience this?

I

With all our perceptions,
there is one thing in common.
One single factor is always present, unvarying.

It is I.
What we are before we add something.

I am ugly, stunning, plain, depressed, smart,
irritated, ecstatic, spiritual, confused. I am...
The list is endless.

Before we can say any of these things,
or come up with zillions of other descriptions,
there has to be first something on which
these descriptions are hooked.

This is the sense of being.
I
Our basic sense of identity.
I
Which has no shape or form or location
or description.
I
The only thing we know about it, is that it Is.
I
This perception I is the first principle.

All else is added.
This IS.
All plays and dances on It, in It, as It.

So deeply spiritual

The thing
with this perspective
is that things are seen just as they are.

And even though we know
we can never catch it in words,
if we do try and just say it as it is,
it is so unlike how society is functioning
that immediately it sounds
so cool,
so deeply spiritual,
so special.

And all we do
is try to describe how it is.

Our natural state.

One thing
I can tell you.

It is the most simple,
the most available thing in the world.

After all,
it is what you are already.

No big deal

One wonders from time to time.

What is the big deal?

After all, it is just the noticing of what is.
What each moment presents itself.

Just a shift from person-oriented seeing
to seeing everything appearing in what we are.

And since it is already the case,
there is nothing neither to be done
nor to achieve.

Just to notice that it is already so.

Effortlessly.

A thunderstorm rolls in with a light show
and lots of noise.
The wind moves the curtains.
The airflow brushes the skin.

Really, no big deal.

When the veils are gone

Through a jungle of words and concepts,
gems are hidden as signposts
to bring the earnest ones home.

∞

Nothing depends on circumstances.

When Life is meant to find completion,
it will do so despite all help and obstacles.

∞

All is the face of the Beloved
when the veils are gone.

Seamless

Sitting here right now
with the fingers dancing
on the keys of the laptop.

An incredible stillness and peace
in which all sounds, sensations
are taking place.

To such an extent that the mind
is quiet, cannot think,
cannot make sense.

An emptiness that takes away anything
personal, located, identified.

It is all one seamless Totality.

One happening.

The easiest way to San Francisco

Confusion, confusion...
Who am I?

Am I the one
who is trying to figure out these nondual words,
trying to understand this ununderstandable message?

Or is the process of trying to understand an automatic
functioning of the mind?

Like the heart is beating and the blood is pumping,
the mind is trying to understand.

As this is what the mind does.
Trying to figure things out,
organize and put them into place.

But then who am I?
And who is asking the question: "Who am I?"

Is it the same mind that wants to know the easiest
way to travel to San Francisco?

You cannot go there, here, with the mind.
You are already here.

Let the mind run and run and meanwhile,
just look and see.

Where are you right now?

And what do you notice?

You notice noticing.

You see seeing happening.

You experience experiencing happening.

This is It...

This is too simple for the mind.
So it will go on a few million more rounds
trying to figure out the unfiguroutable.

And while it goes on, and on and on,
just notice noticing happening,
aware of awaring happening.

Naturally and spontaneously.

Always on.
Always ongoing.
And there is not a someone doing it.

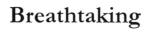

Breathtaking

Whose eyes?

The late afternoon sunlight
shining through the window
reflects on the stone floor,
lights up the whole room.

A solid field of silent stillness
in which all appears.

This open spacious Awareness
is always here.

And when there is recognition
of Awareness with its source,
joy and peace are overwhelming.

Tears in one's eyes.

Whose?

Free fall

When one falls in love with Awareness,
one falls in love with Oneself.

All one is,
is instantaneous,
effortlessly accepted.

And this miraculously includes
everything else as well.

In free fall,
no end to it...

A better deal

What a great invention, red wine.

What great inventions,
all things beautiful and delicious.

What a marvellous adventure, this ride of Life.
With ups and downs.
The thrills and the scary stuff.

Passion, laughter, union, exhilaration.
Anger, pain, depression, loss.

Experiencing the highs and lows,
the mountaintops and the valleys.

A myriad of miracles
happening at each moment.

Why would we deny ourselves the richness of Life?

We limit and protect ourselves, too scared to enjoy.
Looking away from what is in front of our eyes.

How much do we miss out
on the infinite possibilities offered
when we imagine ourselves separate and incomplete.

Not seeing what is here right now.
But looking somewhere else for a better deal.

Perfect

No need to change anything.

It is already the perfect expression.

Whatever form this expression takes.
Be it sweet and gentle or rough and pushy.
Be it storms and cyclones or sunny days.

Could it be any different?

Does the weather have a choice in the way it is?
Do we have a choice in being the way we are?

Feel the incredible benevolence
inherent in accepting
the way things are.

We are already perfect.
Right here right now.

No need to go anywhere.
No need to look anywhere for a brighter future.

Moonlight filtering through the windows.
Coconut leaves rustling in the wind.
The dog on the terrace moaning and howling in
its sleep.

What to say?

Someone asked me today:
'What is God?'

What to say
about everything not leaving out anything?

What to say
about the miracle called Life?

What to say
about that Something that perceives All,
is All but defies any description?

That Something that animates the stars, the atoms,
the renewing of cells, this amazing functioning body.

Look at any tree, anything for that matter.
And we are stunned by the miracle of existence.

Shapes, colours, textures.
Such an amazing array of sensory perceptions
appearing as that Something that cannot be described.

Beyond labels.
Beyond the idea of being a someone.

Surprise, surprise...
We are that Something.

What a show!

The plan is to step into an airplane
in a few days' time
and land on another continent.
A change of scene.
Another set of images
on the screen of Awareness.

Actually we are, all of us,
our own home movie theatre.
With a constant movie running.
Life.

The beauty,
the tragedy,
the boredom,
the drama,
the interactions,
playing out just where we are.

And we have front row seats.
Actually there is only one seat.
There is only one spectator.
Me.

Your Face

All alone with the Beloved meeting us.

In the soft wind and gentle sun on the skin.

In the sound of the motorbike purring.
In the bumps on the road rocking and rolling.
In the bantering with the workers at the pottery
and the delight of the easy contact.
In the bickering with the colleagues
and in the irritation coming up.

The crunching of leaves under the feet.
The whiff of incense in passing the incense factory.
The sight of birds in flight from tree to tree.
The strong presence of tall trees and thick foliage.
In the cramps and queasy feeling in the stomach.

Talks with good friends.
Delicious spinach ricotta pie.

In the stern faces on bikes meeting us.
In the smiles and nods.
In the open and innocent greetings from children.

Pods of cotton on the silk-cotton tree
against the blue sky.

A talk with my sister on Skype.
The screeching windmill.
And dinner standing ready.

Everywhere I meet Your face.

Nowhere are You not.

All is You meeting me as my Self.

For the Love of It.
For the Joy of It.

For You.

Only You
which is Me,
which is Everything.

This is All there Is.

Breathtaking

Every moment is new
and completely open
when we can see It as it is.

Without the luggage of the past.
With the eyes of a child.

An innocence.
A happiness.
Just like that.
Without reason.
Because of Everything.
Because of Nothing.

Shining through.
Without obstruction.

The Divine is not something far away.
It is closer than we think,
closer than our thinking.
More intimate than our own breath.

And it is breathtaking
when we fall together
with the recognition
that we are That already
and always have been.

Sweet silent miracle

The sweet silent miracle
of knowing oneself
to be Self.

And in so knowing,
Knowing All
intimately.

The crowing of a rooster.
A lizard chirping.

The sensation of coolness
where the stone floor meets the foot.

Wafts of smoke drifting in
from the nearby village.

Daybreak and dim shapes
turn into bushes and trees.

It is All You touching Me.

Oh how close you are
My very own Self...

No more veils
to hide Your radiant gaze.

From every corner of the Universe
I see only You seeing Me.

Hither and thither

With not a care in the world,
one is blown
hither and thither.

At times
to lie quiet in some corner,
and then again with the wind
high in the thick of things.

Shaken and moved,
here and there,
up and down,
in different places.
Hush...

And one is moved
or immobile gladly.

As either way
is always
the caress and touch
of the Beloved.

There is no greater joy
than being
a slave of God.

Stillness

Stillness, unmoving, immutable.

Sitting on the back of a motorbike
speeding 100 miles an hour.

Leaning in as the resistance is great.

The wind is tugging
trying to tumble us.

And yet, what I am is still.
Does not move.

The world is passing by.
Rushing.
Swallowing up.
Scene after scene.
Appearing and disappearing.

Seen by what I am.
All is moving in Me.

The conversation

The conversation
this morning where the soft sand gave way
when my bare foot came down,
the dewdrops from the grass
trickle down the ankle,
and the sound of small twigs
break on the forest floor.

The conversation
yesterday at acro yoga
with the weight and delicate finding of ease
as one balances in midair upside down
on some other body's feet.
Not knowing anymore where one body starts
and the other begins.
Only sensations of stretching, balancing
of weight and movement are perceived.
The world seen from unusual angles.

The conversation
at all times ongoing
as we move and see,
hear and smell, taste and touch,
all and everything that appears
in our field of perception.

A fullness and aliveness always there
but rarely noticed in its richness and intensity
as most of our attention stays captivated by
the belief in the reference point we call me.

While at each moment
a million things are going on,
the narration of keeping this me alive
hijacks the direct perception.

The Aliveness without filters.

Stripped

Stripped

One unified field
where nothing is lacking.
And nothing is in excess,
all perfect as it is.

No inside, no outside.
No person, no world.
Just perceiving going on
of that which appears.

No past, no future.
No time, only Now
presently appearing.
Now,
and again Now,
only Now...
And no meaning other than what is.

All these words make it sound
mysterious and unfathomable
but only for the mind.

It is the most simple, natural,
ordinary thing that exists.

It is what we are,
stripped of all labels,
beliefs and concepts,
stripped of the belief in a person.

Unobtrusive

The space, Awareness,
that is our home, our being which
we consciously and unconsciously
always long for
is something so unobtrusive and quiet
that we can easily miss it.

We have been conditioned to override
the awareness of Awareness
by the stories of our life.
We have been taught to forget it,
turn away from what we are
and to believe in a false identity
while all the while it is just here.

It is the quiet noticing of everything.

First to recognize it.
Then get to know it.
Then include everything in it.
As Awareness accepts everything
and has no preferences.

Even to play the story of a person is perfect.
As there is no one bound
and no one to become free.

Pitter-patter

Morning dew.
Dripping drops
on broad leaf plants.
A single bird chirping.

Midday lunch.
Cling-clang of cutlery
and lively conversations
over plates of pasta.

Evening silence.
Brooding.
Fireworks in a distant village.
Howling jackals.

The empty night
swallows all.

There you are...

When sitting relaxed
somewhere
sometime
watching the scene,
whatever it is,
it might happen
that a quietness is noticed
naturally observing
what is there
without strain or tension
without labelling or judging.

Just seeing things as they are.

There you are...

Irrevocably

Your true identity is irrevocably This.

To go and seek awakening shows a misconception,
as what you Are is none other than this wordless
Knowing.

No getting away from It, stop for once.
See and recognize what is always here.
What is always present and aware?

That nameless something in which all is taking place.

The I which is seen as an observer is itself taking place
in this spaceless space.

Look at your own direct experience.
It is the only thing you have.
All else is second hand knowledge through books or
teachers, taken on by believing in it.

Start where you are.
Here and now.
Dismiss all concepts and ideas you have about this.
See and recognize.
Your perceptions are the only thing that matters.
Become intensely interested in your own subjective
experience.

What you are is the ultimate subject.

There is no Other.

There is Nothing outside of This.

Nothing inside either.

It is Full and Empty.
It is All and Nothing.

It is Me.
There is no Other.

All intimately Known
in the Immediacy
by No One.

Life itself

Of all things
the most amazing
is Life itself.

Which is no thing.

Which is all there is.

Which is you.

You are all there is.

There are no clear borders
between what you take yourself to be
and feelings,
thoughts,
perceptions,
the world.

Nothing is demarcated indicating:
"Here is where you stop
and where something else starts."

There is no separation.
Check it out.

It is all happening in the one space which is you.

There you are.

The wheel of life

What do we know?
Really?

Chained to the wheel of life,
our habits, expectations,
beliefs and desires
are propelling us forward
in a rut of our own making
day after day.

Is this why we are here?

No one wants to know?

Where is the wonder, the curiosity?

Questioning everything,
even one's own existence,
especially one's own existence.

Opening up
to whatever
is beyond the conceived limitations
of our own identity.

Wow...

Are we in for a surprise...

Useless words

Feathered seed pods
drift and float in their hundreds
in front of the window.

Small boats with engines
and loud laughter.

Footsteps on a wooden floor.
Sensations in the body.
A thought of a friend.

Always something is noticed,
Always something is ongoing.

Rising up and disappearing again
in this open spaciousness.

Sitting in a bar
or walking in the streets.
Watching a movie
or eyes closed in bed.

Anywhere and everywhere,
this open spaciousness
is the one thing always here.
The one constant in our lives.

No need to go anywhere
or do anything special.

Any idea
that It is not here yet
is only another thought.

Any thought
that our circumstances are not yet good enough,
something needs to be changed or made perfect,
are only strategies of the mind
to avoid and look away.

Do not take my word for it.

Without the actual seeing of This,
they are mere useless words.

The key to Oneness

Oneness can only be perceived
by an uncluttered gaze, by an open view.
Nothing obstructing the immediacy of perceiving.
Touched by all and everything.
This is what we are.

The beauty, the boundless joy.
In wave after wave.
Sat Chit Ananda.

In order to get to the point where Oneness
is known to be what we are, we necessarily have to
come out of the confines, the shackles, the beliefs
that convey to us that we are limited and separate.

The way to free oneself of these bonds
is simply to question.

Is it true?
Am I limited?

Do not take any answer as an easy way out.
Find out.

Touch the walls of your prison.
Do they have a permanent validity?

Am I who I always thought I was?

Who am I?

Life at zero distance

How far do we have to travel?
To which places do we need to go?
What time frame will deliver
the freedom from ourselves?

In a way we all feel something is not right.
We look for happiness somewhere else.
Because where we are, it is not. That is true.

When the identification is not seen through.
When we believe ourselves to be
a someone separate from what is,
the filters in place distort our perceptions.

Life is experienced through a haze of concepts
and ideas.
Life feels limited, predictable and boring.

A daily routine or family set up, a work situation
or our depression and illness, we blame for an
unfulfilled life.

What if for once we question everything?
All labels, beliefs and assumptions.
And inquire into the nature of what we truly are?

The freedom from the idea of being a someone
strips us naked.
And we discover that fulfilment is here and now.

Life at zero distance.

The ruthless Truth

Of Mice and Men

How come we miss the Obvious?

How come the one Changeless factor in our life
escapes our attention?

Absorbed by small life concerns and demands,
we are glued to the ever changing appearances.

One after the other,
rushing in and out.

As on a tread mill.

Willing mice running for our lives
round and round.

It is often when some obstacle happens
to our daily rounds and routines,
some upheaval or accident,
a breakup, sickness or death
that we are stopped in our tracks.

The treadmill slows down.
The rat race is questioned.

Do we dare jump off the wheel?

Willing to disappear to all we have known?

Disappear all together?

Scrambled eggs

Out of the ferns, sliding
silent and smooth.
Two meters long and intense,
across aeons of time.

Shaking out an old bedsheet,
tiny white gecko eggs
tumble and crack open.
Scrambled eggs for breakfast
for hundreds of ants.

It is a rude awakening
to realize there is no enlightenment to get,
nothing to obtain but everything to lose.

This does not mean we can drop the search.
But we are asked to question the premise
that we are a person.

Everything stands
and falls by this identification.

Realizing who and what we are,
we fall into the discovery
of the emptiness of our true Nature
and the fullness of Existence.

Everything is instantly experienced
at no distance from one's Self.

Are we serious?

Are we serious?
Do we want to know the Truth
more than anything?

Provided the need to know the Truth is paramount.
And it is not just to feel good that we are on the path,
we might want to look at this seeking conundrum
in another way:
"Why is this perspective,
what we are, so difficult to see
while all the while we are It already."

This paradox is the most perplexing.
What is the answer?
What is the problem here?
Where do we go off the rails?

It is like the zen koan of Alan Watts:
'Trying to understand God
is like trying to fall in love with a kilometre.'

We are using the wrong tool
to apprehend what is pointed at.
The mind will never get this.

So where does this leave us?

Finding its way through the cracks

Do we feel the urge to step out of the prison?
To question Life?
What is the purpose?
Who am I?

Courageous we are doing this, going against
culture, conditioning, upbringing.

After all some people around us might think
we are a little nuts, not understanding our drive
and passion.

Where are our daring clarity and strength
coming from?
Did we fabricate these in our own little clarity
and strength factory?
Or did we buy them yesterday at the corner
shop?
Where does our urge originate from?

When this message starts to wear down
the vestiges of the identification, and we know
intellectually that the person as such has no
reality, it might dawn that the urge to free
ourselves is freedom itself wanting to remove all
that stands in the way.

There never was a person looking for Freedom.

Freedom is already finding its way through the
cracks.

Kicking the lazy separate self's butt

'There is no doer.' is not the same
as 'There is nothing to do.'

'There is no doer' might be taken by the body-mind,
still under the impression of being a separate entity,
that there is nothing to do.

So the statement 'There is no doer.' is taken as a
concept.
A position is taken in regards to this statement.
The interpretation often leads to passivity,
complacency and a quiet desperation.

'I can't do anything,' is not what is meant.

'There is no doer.' is a description of how it already is.

The invitation is to investigate, to find in our own
experience what this concept is pointing at, whether it
is true.

In a way, the concept 'There is no doer.' asks us to
look, investigate, do something.

It invites the Beingness we are already,
only wrapped up in wrong concepts,
to start questioning the individual we think we are.

If the thirst for reality takes over, it can be intense,
passionate.

And as it takes over more and more, it is seen
and recognized that the Beingness has been
there from beginning to end.

It is the One looking for Itself.

The search is not a person
trying to find Enlightenment.

It is Oneness wriggling Itself out of the confines
and beliefs that tell us right now that we are an
individual, independent and separate.

Actually...

Beingness would love to kick
our lazy separate self's butt seriously.

So we can finally start
questioning this false identity.

The ruthless Truth

The one thing we do not want to hear is that
the search can be dropped right here and now.
As there never has been a pot of gold
at the end of the rainbow.
There will be no enlightenment in the future.

The ruthless Truth is that
the person we believe ourselves to be will never get it.

The pristine Awareness that we are already
does not need any improvement
to be able to comprehend itself.

Freedom is not for the person.
It is freedom from the person.

And...

What we are looking for
is what we are looking from.

But then, who knows?

Even though we do not want to hear this,
it might be that Awareness,
trying to recognize Itself through us,
drops this information in our lap
so we, after investigating this belief
of being a person and seeing the fallacy of it,
might finally relax, sit back and enjoy the show...

Final

Let go of all that tells you
that you are
limited,
personal,
located.

That you are
incomplete,
separate,
bound.

How?

There is no how.

You have to look for yourself.

Is there any truth
in these beliefs and ideas?

A passion to find out
is all you need.

Keep looking...

The end of a journey

One spring afternoon in 2009, the last piece of the puzzle found its place, effortlessly.

Walking away from meeting Leo Hartong in Holland, his simple words "Yes, this is It," had once and for all confirmed the answers to my questions: " Is it the Beingness of what we are?", "Is it what the search is about?", "Is it really this simple?"

The simplicity of the information stared at me as I made my way back to the train station.

It stared at the trees lining the streets and the people walking and shopping. Nothing had changed and yet everything was different, direct, immediate.

Not that I did not know this intimacy. I had been having Oneness experiences in which the child, the adolescent, the adult disappeared and the thing that remained was the field of awareness with sounds, sights and smells in vibrant clarity.

Only, it had taken a 25 year journey to come to this understanding.

While I boarded the train, I wondered how come this obviousness had not been recognized before, how could I have been so dense that I had failed to notice it, while it stared at me right in the face all this time.

I grew up in a large Catholic family in a village in Holland. Both my parents worked hard to earn the financial means to raise seven children. This left them little time to further instruct and condition their brood.

The religious background, as lived by my family, was one of accepting and following. We children did not ask questions, and primary school with 45 children in one class did not help to inspire a thirst for knowledge.

These factors contributed to an unquestioning mind. Not that the child was dumb, I was quick to learn, but education as it was presented held no particular interest.

There were Oneness experiences from time to time but as they had been there always, they were seen as a natural part of life. I thought everyone had those experiences and did not talk about them. How could I have talked about something that defies description?

Out of a wish to help others, I trained as a nurse. I also went travelling for a few years. And life went on.

Even when the spiritual journey started at age 22 reading spiritual books, there was no recognition upon reading similar experiences others had had, or going through teachers' descriptions about the intimacy of being. My Oneness experiences were ordinary, while the Oneness experiences in the books sounded special, something to strive for.

It is not that these immediate perceptions were not known. Something was not yet perceived.

By 1984, I had settled in the international township of Auroville in South India where, by the mere fact of living there, national and religious conditioning fell away. Other identifications were seen through by trying to follow the teachings of Sri Aurobindo and the Mother. Through observing and watching the mind, emotions and body: "Neti neti: I am not the mind, I am not the emotions, I am not the body." And through practicing the ways of Bhakti and Karma yoga, the conditioning of the body-mind thinned out.

It was a natural process with no particular aim in mind. There was no person seeking happiness or looking for enlightenment. If at all, there was more the wish to surrender to something vaster. And there was still the vague idea of a permanent state of bliss in a distant future.

There were at times periods of silence and joy, but these came and went. Often I wondered what was going on.

There had always been a resonance with the truth of these teachings, but often the language was far too abstract for this lazy mind of mine that had skipped over the parts that might have shortened the journey.

Of course, the seeking journey of Anamika was perfect because this is what happened. Oneness seeking itself through a meandering sort of way...

A few years before the recognition, Oneness must have felt that enough is enough. And expressed the need for a conclusion.

Perhaps in order that recognition could take place, the urge to exercise the mind appeared out of nowhere. There also came the realization that the mind was lazy and the need to occupy it came up.
Along with the reading of difficult philosophical books, learning accounting started, as well as playing games on the computer to make the mind more alert, pliable, concentrated.

At this time, I also discovered the Internet and a whole world opened up.
I was introduced to modern day nonduality teachers who were my age and spoke my language.
It suddenly became accessible.

Only at this point with recognition so close, did the desire for liberation wake up. And a passion to Know appeared.

Clarity was there.
What these teachers were talking about was already operating in my life, but there was the disbelief that It could be so simple.

I needed the confirmation of someone whom I could fully trust, who would be able to confirm the insane premonition 'I Am what I am looking for'.
This is when I asked Leo Hartong if we could meet.

That afternoon in 2009, while looking for a vacant seat in a compartment, I came to realize that these last years' experiences of not feeling like a person, and the thought that something was wrong were not the signs of a mental breakdown but the delicate perfume of the Infinite.

As the train made its way back to Amsterdam through a landscape of meadows and suburbs, there came the realization, the Knowing, that the key is neither the Oneness experiences nor the deconditioning process, as both do not necessarily deliver the conclusion.
The One thing, the missing key is the recognition of Beingness, the simple fact of Existing.

The train arrived at Central station.
And so it was the end of the journey.
(Of course, it is understood this is only a story.)

> *When the mind is at peace,*
> *the world too is at peace.*
> *Nothing real,*
> *nothing absent.*
> *Not holding on to reality,*
> *not getting stuck in the void,*
> *you are neither holy nor wise,*
> *just an ordinary fellow who has completed his work.*

- P'ANG YUN (HO UN)

Acknowledgments

I wish to thank all people, influences, happenings, accidents and calamities seen and unseen who have guided this journey.

Deep gratitude to Didier Weiss for sorting out and selecting the original posts from the blog "Potshots"; Cécilia Weiss for her untiring dedication towards editing the texts, layout and book design; both of them for their support, expertise, countless lunches, cups of coffee, drinks, wonderful talks and lots of laughter; Navoditte, Deepak Balachandran and Anand Shanti for their suggestions and proofreading; Emily Goodman for the portrait; Ogy Enev for the photographs "Emptiness", "Heaven is now", "Stripped" and the front & back cover.

Special thanks to Jerry Katz who has been a guiding light since we met.

Oneness taking the shape of gratitude.

Do not believe anything written here.
These are all concepts.
All second hand information.
No use to anybody.

And while we are here looking for something
Life is happening anyway.